This Persistent Gravity

poems by

Angie Crea O'Neal

Finishing Line Press
Georgetown, Kentucky

This Persistent Gravity

Copyright © 2023 by Angie Crea O'Neal
ISBN 979-8-88838-124-3 First Edition
All rights reserved under International and Pan-American Copyright Conventions. No part of this book may be reproduced in any manner whatsoever without written permission from the publisher, except in the case of brief quotations embodied in critical articles and reviews.

ACKNOWLEDGMENTS

Anchor & Plume Press: *The Way Things Fall* (chapbook)
River Teeth Journal's "Beautiful Things" Series: "Paradise Lost" and "Atlantis"
Cumberland River Review: "Ezekiel"; "When the moon tells us of losses"; and "The Valley"
Stirring: "Imago"
Sycamore Review: "Pieces"
The Chimes: "Mont Blanc" (under the title "One"); "Gomer Goes Home"; and "Kayaking"
Kindred: "Laundry" and "Deus Ex Machina"
Psaltery & Lyre: "The Milky Way" and "The Anniversary"
Perspectives Journal: "Gardensong" and "Hosea, Single"
The Windhover: "God Speaks"
San Pedro River Review: "Theodicy" and "The Law of Falling Bodies"
Kentucky Review: "The Prophet" and "Extinction"
Gravel: "Maricopa County Fair"
Relief: A Journal of Art and Faith: "Empty Nesting" and "Notes on Deism"
The Christian Century: "After the Iridotomy"
Calla Press: "The Good Snake"; "Against Love Poetry"; and "Fixer-Upper"

Publisher: Leah Huete de Maines
Editor: Christen Kincaid
Cover Art: Whitney Schlander
Author Photo: Fabrice Poussin
Cover Design: Elizabeth Maines McCleavy

Order online: www.finishinglinepress.com
also available on amazon.com

Author inquiries and mail orders:
Finishing Line Press
P. O. Box 1626
Georgetown, Kentucky 40324
U. S. A.

Table of Contents

Paradise Lost 1

Ezekiel 2

Imago 3

Pieces 4

In Middle Age 11

After the Iridotomy 12

When the moon tells us about losses 13

Thirteen 14

St. George Island, 1984 15

Orbit 17

The Way Things Fall 19

Tomorrow Island 23

The Valley 24

Mont Blanc 25

Notes on Deism 26

Maricopa County Fair 28

Laundry 29

Tintern Abbey 30

Hosea plays in the rain 31

Extinction 32

Kayaking 34

Deus Ex Machina 36

The Milky Way 38

Clocks 39

Gardensong 40

The Mistress 41

Against Love Poetry 43

The Good Snake 44

Theodicy 45

Fixer-Upper	47
God Speaks	48
The Prophet	49
Eight	50
The Anniversary	51
On Learning Einstein Was Divorced on Valentine's Day	52
Gomer Goes Home	53
Entropy	54
I Write	55
All the Light	56
Kingdom Come	59
Atlantis	61
Empty Nesting	62
The Law of Falling Bodies	63
This Persistent Gravity	64
Hosea, Single	67

for my father
James Robert Nicholson Crea (1934-2021)

"Philosophy is written in this grand book—I mean universe—which stands continuously open to our gaze, but which cannot be understood unless one first learns to comprehend the language in which it is written. It is written in the language of mathematics, and its characters are triangles, circles and other geometric figures, without which it is humanly impossible to understand a single word of it; without these, one is wandering about in a dark labyrinth."

Galileo (1623)

"The poet ventures to make sensible rational ideas of invisible beings… sensible beyond the limits of experience, with a completeness that goes beyond anything which there is an example in nature."

Immanuel Kant (1790)

"I will plant her for myself in the land;
I will show my love to the one I called 'Not my loved one.'
I will say to those called 'Not my people,' 'You are my people';
and they will say, 'You are my God.'"

Hosea 2:23

Paradise Lost

My daughter spies it first, the butterfly limp on the pavement. She pleads to move it since the path, bordering the river, is crowded in late summer. I try my old tricks of distraction, the ones that always worked. What if it's just sleeping, I muse, *like Jacob on his pillow of stones?*

But she's nine now and knows.

I look east, over her shoulder, and imagine a cicada crawling back into its skin, molted wings furled against a grain of morning. Far from the elm, it burrows, returning deep for day into the mud below. And by the river, flagging branches that hang their rotted tips like fingers in the current are restored to technicolor green, like it was in the spring, before the wing-flitted body learned to plunder, conformed to the excesses of nature, its wings cutting a blank sheet of sky obliquely, consequence of flight the curse of indirection.

We get to work—dodging bikers, bearing the humidity like penitents—and using a dried magnolia leaf as a makeshift stretcher, lift its crumpled body over to a safer spot in the shade. It's the best we can do, and so we make our solitary way, still carrying the weight of its suffering between us under the light of an incriminating sun.

But, *what else could hold us together, love,* I whisper like a prayer. What else could bring water from the stone, break the tender mollusk of our heart open from its shell?

Ezekiel

College Park, Georgia

Climb the streets of your first town, the one that still lives in the rill of time, there in the melting blue before rivers. Go back and make snow angels in the shallow dusting of thought, swing on the branches of unknowing. Revisit and eat the scrolls that tell the story of your youth. Search for old friends hanging on memory like gossamer, tell them what you've learned, confess to them your faults.

Whisper all you've lost and retreat to those early places to feel the weight of the sturdy wood beneath, wrapped tight in a soft lawn of cotton blanket. Recall the hours scrubbing dirt from your fingers, splinters coaxed from skin with tweezers. Don't forget about the pine straw pillows, no fear of ditchwater, those close encounters under a broken porch light. Walk roads with names you no longer remember

and wander along dirt paths that lead to forest dells, drop sticks in the creek and watch them float east, towards the center. Retrace your steps and find rest under a thick quilt of forgetting like a strong arm nestled in the arch of your back. Climb the streets of your childhood, the place that still holds you, haunts you like a dream, like a close, constant hand on your shoulder.

Imago

Remember the thick-pined
woods behind the old chicken
coop? How we swept

the forest floor looking
for golf balls lost from the
course next door; the joy of
finding one submerged in
the litterfall of longleaf pines
like a forlorn Easter egg—
childish logic, having such
faith in what we could hold,
how many cicada shells we
could carry from the deep,
cached in coffers brimmed
with summer.

We only heard the thrumming
music of bodies; never noticed
day molting its golden shade,
sky unloosened, emptying its
harvest in the curve of light

shadows breaking beneath
shoots of wings, thin as timbal.

Her voice, calling us
home—

how, in time, we'd learn to see
such grace in the world: last light
unfastening the dark, setting
us back into our shells,

wingless out of rust-buckets
undone, we'd fly like wonder
from the hollow trees.

Pieces

> "Arrange whatever pieces come your way."
> —Virginia Woolf

Synchronicity (noun): "the simultaneous occurrence of events that appear significantly related but have no discernible causal connection."

*

In hindsight, the sunglasses he always wore in his online pics should have been a sign. Take the one of him standing by the Jeep stranded in the creek, off-roading gone wrong, looking athwart like an obdurate captain surveying the sea. Mysterious, I thought, yet capable. The kind of man who could help a divorced single-mom in a pinch.

*

The expression "in a pinch" dates back to the 1400s and means "in an emergency" or "when hard-pressed."

*

My marriage ended abruptly one Sunday afternoon after church.

*

Joel 2:25: "I will give you back what you lost to the swarming locusts, the hopping locusts, the stripping locusts, and the cutting locusts. It was I who sent this great destroying army against you."

*

I don't know much about locusts, but I know random facts about mayflies, thanks to summers on Lake Huron. Buried in up to 48 feet of lake sediment, it takes mayfly eggs two years to mature and hatch. Once born, they manage to find their way up and out of the water (a sight that must be) only to live 24 hours. A lot of effort for a day.

*

I'm reading the entire Bible chronologically and am in the book of Leviticus, which reads like a mouthful of saltine crackers. Much of the Old Testament is thunderous and retributive, like nature "red in tooth and claw" as Tennyson said.

*

Shortly after my divorce, I discovered John Milton's sonnet, "When I consider how my light is spent." I had long marveled at *Paradise Lost*, overwhelmed by its scope, Milton an intellectual giant for the ages. I've admired him as a tourist does a cultural landmark, slack-jawed and cautious. But that sonnet wasn't written by Milton, the one-name literary icon, composer of epics, but by a man with two names, a sonneteer who found himself at odds with the life he was given, nearly undone by failure (including going blind at 43).

He wrote that sonnet not to pontificate, but to process.

*

In 2016, a rare eyeless catfish was discovered in a limestone cave deep in an aquifer underlying the Rio Grande basin. The slow-moving Mexican blindcat adapted to an environment so remote eyesight was unnecessary. One scientist explains how these strange creatures honed "extra-sensory abilities to succeed in total darkness."

*

Milton composed *Paradise Lost* by "extra-sensory" means, waking and dictating lines that he had dreamt the night before to his daughters, who became his scribes. Incidentally, his domestic life was a mess. He had three wives, two of whom died in childbirth, and was reportedly tyrannical and emotionally abusive to his daughters.

*

Gerard Manly Hopkins, a poet with three names who never married and lived some 200 years after Milton, wrote a famous sonnet as well: "The world is charged with the grandeur of God/It will flame out, like shining from shook foil;/It gathers to a greatness, like the ooze of oil/Crushed." When I teach this poem, I remind my students that the ancient world used olives for virtually everything from medicine to lamp fuel. *But the olives had to be hard pressed and crushed to be of greater value.*

*

I read that the Hopkins' family motto was *esse quan videri*, "To be rather than to seem."

*

I suppose "catfished" is the technical term for what happened to me. In hindsight, the only thing I knew to be true about the sunglassed man was his job as a fireman. He once told me an elaborate tale wherein he nearly died fighting a house fire to play on my sympathies, get me to the altar faster.

*

Milton wasn't a giant; he was just a man who was, at times, afraid. "And that one talent which is death to hide/Lodged with me useless," he wrote, fearing his disability would be the end of his career.

*

"Good and bad men are less than they seem." Samuel Taylor Coleridge

*

Later in life, plagued with doubt and depression and likely suffering from bipolar disorder, Hopkins wrote a series of sonnets named "the terrible sonnets" for their evocation of deep despair and sorrow.

In one of these, Hopkins asks of God: "But ah, but O thou terrible, why wouldst thou rude on me/Thy wring-world right foot rock? lay a lionlimb against me? Scan/With darksome devouring eyes my bruisèd bones?"

*

One of Hopkins' friends, John Bayley, wrote of him (I read this on Wikipedia): "All his life Hopkins was haunted by the sense of personal bankruptcy and impotence, the straining of 'time's eunuch' with no more to 'spend'...a sense of inadequacy."

*

French psychoanalyst Jacque Lacan believed we are all chasing a lost object of desire, namely the repressed desire for wholeness that we once had in an idealized union with our mother.

*

I don't know what the mayflies are chasing during their day, probably the light.

*

I worry about being a good mother. Once when my daughters were small, my emotions flew out of orbit, and I tried to run away. I got halfway to the end of the street before I saw them in the rear-view mirror on the porch, holding onto each other like two birds huddled on a wire.

*

In psychotherapy, *imago* means an idealized image of someone, usually a parent, that influences a person's behavior. In entomology, it means the final, mature stage of a winged insect. In Hebrew, "imago dei" means that we are created in the image of God.

*

Hopkins sketched a self-portrait once and called it "Gerard Hopkins, reflected in a Lake." He appears to be sitting on the edge of a dock, legs dangling, fully clothed with a bowler hat, staring down at his reflection. But he's no Narcissus. There's existential melancholy in the muted figure that stares back, as if he's looking, not at himself, but at the world through breathed-on glass.

*

Most of his poems were not published until after his death.

*

A curious thing: when I first saw Hopkins' portrait, almost like a Rorschach test, I thought it was abstract—as if he went to sit down and someone pulled the chair from underneath him, and he began to fall off the edge of that lake, as if such a thing could happen, knees to nose, body sinking into the horizon.

*

I know it's possible, by the way, to fall off the edge of your life, to feel the weight that brings the shelf down, the sturdy wood you know is there suddenly becoming air.

*

Mayflies are members of a species of insects called "ephemeroptera" from the Greek word "ephemeros" meaning "short-lived."

*

I take too many selfies. I don't post them anywhere, so I'm unsure what purpose they serve other than to prove to myself that I'm still here.

*

I've always thought the best thing about having an identical twin would be knowing what I really look like from the outside in. Even then, would I believe what I saw, consider it evidence that I'm okay?

*

The English empiricist John Locke argued all ideas come from sensory experience. But, no one has ever said to me, *you're unlovable*.

*

Lacan called the psychological stage when we feel the most complete and inseparable from our environment the *Mirror Stage*—preverbal and driven by image, in a time before our fall into language and division. He associated this stage with the Imaginary Order.

*

What if selfies, like self-portraits, aren't shallow at all but a latent desire for the lost paradise of our mother?

*

Speaking of latent, did you know cicadas live underground for nearly 17 years before they see the light of day?

*

Did you know this essay was rejected 17 times before it was accepted for publication?

*

The fireman I thought would rescue me like a cat stuck in a tree once said, "what makes you think anyone else would want to read what you write?"

*

In *Biographia Literaria*, S.T. Coleridge says the secondary imagination is that quality of mind which "dissolves, dissipates, in order to re-create; or where this process is rendered impossible, yet still at all events it struggles to idealize and to unify."

*

Hopkins described his "terrible sonnets" as the "thin gleanings of a long weary while."

*

Once exposed, the fireman I met online abandoned his plan and went away. My life is not the plot of a romantic *Lifetime* movie.

*

Recently, I rescued two abandoned dogs stranded at a church on Highway 92, an adult female and a male pup. I'm sure she's the mom. She had a familiar look that day, a mix between anguish and resolve, world-weariness. I carried those dogs to my car without thinking and took them home because they needed me.

*

Did you know the Wood Boring Beetle can live up to 50 years?

*

"And for all this," Hopkins wrote, "nature is never spent;/There lives the dearest freshness deep down things."

*

Coincidentally, the first two literary journals that accepted my work sent the news on Sunday mornings, a week apart. One piece was titled, "Theodicy."

*

Coleridge believed the creative imagination was "esemplastic," from the Greek *eh hen*, meaning "into one."

*

Sometimes God sends the locusts, and sometimes he sends a poem.

*

"God doth not need/Either man's work or his own gifts; who best/Bear His mild yoke, they serve Him best." Milton

*

I have been surprised to find passages of lyrical beauty in the Old Testament: "Command the children of Israel, that they bring unto thee pure oil olive *beaten for the light,* to cause the lamps to burn continually" (Leviticus 24:2).

*

Mark Strand once wrote, "We all have reasons/for moving./I move/to keep things whole."

*

Shortly after bringing her home, we noticed the mom dog often stared blankly into the air. We worried something might be wrong until we realized she was looking for light: the reflection from a wristwatch, metal pots and pans, my iPhone screen sending flashes and beams bouncing like "shining from shook foil" across the kitchen walls, shooting stars.

In Middle Age

my body is an abacus, a calculation
with no numbers. Its root word is sand.
I study it like a prophecy.

In middle age, my body can predict
the rain. Tells time like a toddler,
clicks on at 2am with the furnace.
Measures atmospheric pressure
in my eyes. My body is Grand Central
Station without any trains.

Some days I'm a scientist
searching the universe for
gravitational waves, some echo
of lost sound rippling back from
space like a bell. But, I'm only
standing on its porch, knocking
at my own front door.

Other days I'm a castaway,
scribbling with my finger on its shore.
It's a raft made of driftwood, taking
me past the waves to a city pool where
children play Marco Polo.

In middle age, I'm trying to touch the
bottom of the deep end underneath all
those years before my body rises like a
buoy. Until I rise like a mayfly—from
the root word *ephemera*—breaking time
open like a prophecy.

After the Iridotomy

I tell him my favorite poet went blind at 43,
some think from the same condition as mine.
What good fortune that I can prevent such a loss,
unlike poor Milton whose eyes flickered for years
before they burned out like a candle in middle age.
How I've felt my age mostly in my eyes, as if they
are the center of my gravity, carrying the weight of
getting old like a pair of sore shoulders. So much
looking has made me see less, I say, like reading a
digital clock in the sun. He tells me the iris is just a
muscle controlling the light. I tell him it's color,
named for the Greek goddess who brought the world
messages from the divine. I tell him that Milton
wrote his greatest poem in the dark.

When the moon tells us about losses

> "The moon tells us how great has been its loss,
> as it recovers its full form; its greater losses you
> are already accustomed to measure in a
> mirror of water"
> —Tertullian

Out of the corner of my eye, I think it's a small envelope
caught in an upturn of wind. The luna moth looks
wan and paper thin, mantle of night lost like a tarp unmoored
by driving rain. Last hours of fast living. On the side of my
ramshackle shed in the half-glow of late day, shadows
play. Sumac leaves flash back against the blank screen.
They dance like excess digits on a ledger, opposing the
calculating logic of nature that takes what it wishes—
intractable as late fees, hollow as an empty mailbox. I use
the unpaid bill on the kitchen table as a stretcher, its sturdy
edge carries her to an ocean of open grasses.

A buoy marks the spot where she last played when she went
under, off the shore of a Texas bay, the little girl last summer.
Taken to dark waters by tidal currents as the numbers drop
to zero. I look west. The cows in the pasture across from the
seawall maintain their muted graze, like stranded sailboats
silent under a complicit sky.

Thirteen

These days, you are a city of one-way streets.
Opaque as an urban river, the swell of your current
rising. Childhood left on my shore in a heap
of tangled memories like flotsam.

Was it not yesterday, my love, when your new
moon alone could illume my darkest corners?

Now you are a map of capillary ways, routes too
fresh to bear the weight of direction. Illegible.
At times, an apparition.

Where have you gone amidst your half-glow of electric din?

I, these days, superannuated and circling from a distance,
a tourist witnessing the spectacle from some great height.

You, a skyscraper under a blanket of stars invisible, blinded
by your own light. Stars still overhead, though you can no
longer see them, these days.

St. George Island, 1984

after Wordsworth

"…memory shapes its own Eden within."
—Jorge Luis Borges

When the world is too much
with you, go cry a river. Then
follow its waters to where sea
meadows hold sway in the shallows.

Find the place where current meets
tide, run your fingers through sedge
grasses, slide your wounds like
sore feet into the brackish blue.

Soak the pain off like a stubborn
label, watch your toes wrinkle and
pretend you're growing older.

Remember collecting coquina shells
one summer with your brother,
disembodied wings like angels
glued to poster board, taxonomy of wishes.

Wander into waist-deep water but
no further, hear the plaintive
cries of your mother who shovels
sand dunes, searching for missing children.

Ride the waves until you wash ashore
draped in seaweed, lost mermaid waiting
for Tom Hanks to save you. Sidestep

jellyfish, inside-out like discarded garments
littering the seashore. Try forgetting the fear of
them below you, gaping closet doors in the

darkness. Make a trough deep enough to
drown your feet with sorrows, believe that
if you dig far enough, you might reach China.

Imagine driftwood is sunken treasure
resurrected, its weight straining the plastic
handle of your bucket full of wonder.

Watch your parents grow young in the
surf, wrapping kids in dry towels,
rubbing sand from nether places,
holding it all together. Your body a planet
orbiting their sun.

As a new moon tugs the tide back like
a blanket taken in the night, slipping off the
edge of your world in its turning.

Orbit

> "...run your mind up to heaven by heaven to Him who
> is really the centre, to your senses the circumference,
> of all; the quarry to whom all these huntsmen pursue,
> the candle to whom all these moths move
> yet are not burned."
> —C.S. Lewis, *The Discarded Image*

I'm ten-years old, and we're outside
before daylight, my dad and I bundled up
against the cold March air, on our driveway

beside the wild hedgerow that separates
us from our neighbor, not far from the
canopy of our yew tree outside the
kitchen window.

He likes to remind me that the oldest tree
in Europe is a Fortingall yew, standing
resolute in a Scottish churchyard for 3,000
years. That Pontius Pilate played
        beneath
                its branches.

This morning we watch the planets all lined
up beside the moon like Roman soldiers, rare
astronomical event. I eclipse them with the
        tip of my finger.

Secure in the unconsciousness of childhood,
I miss the fear-mongering on the news,
apocalyptic visions of earthquakes as far as
California portending disaster.

I see only tiny orbs tinged with color, universe
wide-gaping, its coat blown
        open by
                cosmic winds.

Everyone else sleeping through Armageddon,
the event quiet as the Earth's rotation.

I don't notice how tired my dad must be, just
back from the night shift unloading airplanes,
body braced stiff as a collar against the wind.
All the things I don't see when I am ten and the
world orbits
        around me:
                a father's rough hands,
a life stretched out before me like unanswered prayer.

The way day and night contend on lunar plains.

How I turn and follow him back to the house,
celestial bodies moving toward the lamp-lit
kitchen like moths,
        pale as moon,
circling the light.

The Way Things Fall

It was a harrowing flight across the Rockies with my dad in a small Northwest airlines commuter plane. I've had a lifelong fear of falling that has matured into a phobia of everything from roller coasters to vertiginous observation decks. That day I was nearly undone by how plastic the plane sounded as it bounced sharply through pockets of wild air. Each movement was a hard right-angle, and the overhead bins rattled violently. I glanced over and saw my dad sitting beside me, his newspaper folded neatly in a square, still working his crossword puzzle with an ink pen.

When we landed safely in Kalispell, Montana, I half expected to take the next leg of the journey in a covered wagon. Out there all I could see was land and sky—advancing expanses and outstretches so lovely and perilous they seemed not a part of the scene but the whole. As we drove north towards Glacier National Park, the plains gave way to hills, the hills mingled with mountains, and then mountains became monuments. They were the highest I had ever seen, standing like shadowed icons in the twilight. I pressed my nose against the car window, and even though it was June, I could feel the cold night pressing back against the glass.

I had fevered dreams that night about lots of things: falling airplanes, cold summer air, snow-capped mountains, my father reading maps and working puzzles. But I dreamt mostly of land.

*

I spent the summer before my twentieth birthday in Montana, under big skies, chasing the wind.

We lived in groups of four in rustic, tin-roof cabins and were warned not to leave them at night since grizzlies were known to visit the camp when things were dark.

The idea that the most fearsome mammal on earth lived in the woods behind my cabin pierced my soul. I did many things out of character that summer:

I climbed Mt. Henkel, elevation 8,770 feet.

I wore Birkenstocks with socks and Patagonia fleece jackets in July.
I stopped shaving my legs.
I drank whole milk and picked wild huckleberries.
I had a roommate named Clover.

I collected coins from my waitressing tips in a crumpled brown paper bag to use at the pay phones outside Swiftcurrent Motor Inn, and I would stand at the phone booth in my polyester uniform with my paper bag for an hour at a time, feeding it coins, whispering to a boy in Chicago under the dim light of a crescent moon.

I felt infinite in a summer filled with so much land and sky.

*

They say glacial erosion created Swiftcurrent Lake,
centuries of melting and moving water from nearby
Grinnell Glacier creating a cobalt basin, nature seemingly
standing still while the inexorable movement of water carved
beauty 2,000 feet deep.

Sometimes things fall suddenly and all at once, and other times the deepest change moves imperceptibly, hidden beneath the surface under the weight of so much water.

Nature teaches us to tolerate such mystery.

*

Pitamakan Pass was named after an 18th-century female warrior
from the Blackfeet Nation who had a vision quest nearby,
the only woman in her tribe given a man's name.

I wonder what mysterious visions rendered her strong as flint.
And I imagine where she might have stood when prophesy anointed her on those remote and solitary paths. Maybe I stood in that same spot. I think now of Percy Shelley's desire, like Pitamakan,
to find "the everlasting universe of things/where from secret springs/
The source of human thought its tribute brings."

*

I wasn't thinking about poetry when I walked the switchbacks toward
Pitamakan Pass on a hot August day in the summer of 1991 when I was only 19.
Climbing those switchbacks that day took some of my spirit, and I longed
for home. Through wafts of earth and grit, I thought I smelled black coffee,
even sweet confection sprinkled on an Indian taco. My lungs were burning
when we finally stopped to admire Flinsch Peak above Old Man Lake.

The peak is a Matterhorn with an impressive horned shape
that juts from the ridge, pointing to the heavens. Carved out by
several glaciers, it forms a summit with a sharp, narrow point.
It looked like those who summited would be balancing precariously
on the tip of a rustic needle.

We were straddling the Continental Divide, on top of the world,
walking along a watershed with one foot
in the east and one in the west.

There, I could feel pockets of colder air blowing across patches
of unmelted snow and alpine lakes below, and I began to revive.
I think Pitamakan's power must have come from standing on that fulcrum
from whence the waters flow.

*

None of us had never hitchhiked before, but we descended the Pass too late to get to camp before dark.

Our first ride was with a family of American Indians, piled up in the bed of their red pick-up truck like worn tires, before we put our thumbs in the wind again. Then a Volkswagen van, a cliché on wheels, stopped after an hour of us waiting and walking down the highway like a herd of lost mountain goats. The road to St. Mary Valley was straight and flat, but my legs were tired of wandering.

I heard music, maybe Jackson Browne. He sang of walking. I might have hummed along…

And I keep moving, moving on
Things are bound to be improving these days

I sat backpacked, knees to my chin, wrapped in cool wind, as I took in the remains of the day: child of the 80's huddled in a love van and in the presence of hippies, out of place and time.

We were wild with youth, cheating gravity, and I barely felt the weight of the tires on the pavement as we floated towards the valley. I looked out the window, the kind that slides sideways, like the ones on old school buses. The silver moon cast a shadow on an open meadow, its grasses blown back to reveal a trace of amber inside. Fall was coming early in the mountains, and everything seemed poised for change.

*

We pulled into the parking lot at camp, piled out of the hippie van, and joked as we headed to the kitchen for a snack. I could feel the grit of the trails beneath my feet as I climbed into my bunk.

I slept like the dead that night, and I dreamt about the grizzlies in the hills behind our cabins.

Tomorrow Island

My father talks mostly about Alaska now.
How he lived on an Army base on
St. Lawrence Island during the Cold War
where he looked for Russian submarines,

read Morse codes like riddles from a lonely
lip of land in the middle of the sea. I think that

makes my father a spy. He slept in a Quonset
hut shaped like the ribcage of a beached whale,
burned coal and sticks inside that hollow tin can

of a home. He says the island is what remains of
a land bridge that connected Asia and North
America long ago. So many invisible borders up
there: the Aleutian Islands rising like a Sphinx

in the place where east becomes west, or the date
line that runs right between the Diomede Islands

further north, where there's only two miles between
Russia and the U.S. Big Diomede is called "Tomorrow
Island," the little one on the Alaskan side,

"Yesterday Isle." I suppose for the people living on
that little island now, huddled in an area of about two
square miles, looking west across the Bering Strait means
they can see the next day.

I don't want to look that way. I want to stay here with my father
hunched over his morning crossword, his body a waterfall frozen

stiff with ice, telling me again about being young on
a lonely lip of land in the middle of a sea that was
once a bridge, of all things.

The Valley

Matthew 7:26

There never was a marriage. Only
a pack of coyotes bunking in the

foothills behind our house, taking
housecats into brittlebush, pools

tepid as bathwater. There were
mountains shaped like camel humps

made of rocks the color of Mars.
There were rings of desert lavender

to repel scorpions around a house
made of stucco which is made

of sand that would descend like a hell of
bricks during a haboob. There were

cactus wrens making homes in hard places
while we walked the canals at sunset.

There never really was a marriage,
only long walks on canals lined with

saguaros while rock pigeons made nests
in our attic and coyotes nosed the

foothills behind houses made of sand.
Not a marriage, just snow-capped mountains

glinting in the distance like a mirage.
Just the miracle of walks along desert canals

full of melted snow. Walks in the valley, the
place where all the rivers go.

Mont Blanc

after Percy Shelley

I read somewhere we spend thirty
minutes as a single cell. Primal then
as algae. Still as ice in the shallows
of an ancient blue.

That is how we all begin, a rill of
snowmelt at inception before the
riverbed's deepening channel.

One hair of root beneath the earth,
dark over deep in a belly of dirt,
waiting to be born.

And that is where we tend, towards
those thirty minutes of oneness before
rivers, before the predawn fire wakes us

and we run. Back to one where we spot
tadpoles in the basin water, a shard of fossil
lost silent in the mud, a veil of gossamer on

the morning. Back to paying attention as
we listen for the lonesome shrill of a night
train in the distance, its promise of going home.

Notes on Deism

Forget about running with scissors. It's always the thing you'd least expect.

I once saw a tire fly off the back of a semi-truck, cross a busy intersection like Halley's Comet, and tear into a Starbucks parking lot, stopped only by an empty minivan. Then, the story from this past March about a college student on spring break killed by a runaway tire at a rest stop off I-75.

But I still had the handyman tether the new trampoline to the ground in four places. Sandbags wouldn't be enough, I said, to keep the behemoth death-trap from flying, a gusty swell sending it aloft—like those bouncy-house horrors on the news, innocence careening into fences and power lines, a giant Sponge-Bob-shaped hand crushing the world beneath like a clumsy toddler.

Sometimes my mother-heart feels like it's standing under an umbrella that's been sucked up and inside out by the wind. Sometimes I want to make them a long list of precautions, tuck it into their pockets like fairy dust, sew it into the lining of their jackets: avoid left-hand turns with no arrow. Back roads are always safer, except late at night when you should look for the streetlight like the Little Dipper. Don't ever go more than knee-deep in the ocean. If you hear thunder, for the love of God, take cover...

We saw lightning in sunshine last summer at Calloway Gardens. My youngest on the inflatable playground in the middle of the water moving in slow motion because of her life jacket, my frantic pleas for her to hurry must have seemed ridiculous. She doesn't know yet that it's always going to be the freakish thing you least expect like the time long ago when her dad and I were still married and got stuck in Tucumcari, New Mexico in an April blizzard. Spent a night in our car afraid to sleep lest we'd be found like frozen mastodons days later.

Maybe it's middle age or because I have teenagers, but life feels rickety and narrow as a covered bridge. Thin as a margin. Less these days like a page and more like a comma. More like a cell than a body, like back when hope was a cluster of wishes buried inside me.

How foolish to think we could go on like that after, souls now stranded on the curb of reality. As if birth itself isn't the great catastrophe we all fear will send us flying, the flash of oncoming headlights on a back road, the wheel on gravel. Maybe just the college application.

The force that loosens the lug nut and sets it all in motion is the spring storm that comes out of nowhere and takes all the tulips. Mothers are the prophets waving their arms like staffs at all the water and wind. Walking through the whole world like it's a dry riverbed, reaching behind for a hand.

Maricopa County Fair

He hands me his glasses as he walks away towards the carnival lights. I hold the stems gingerly to protect the glass, my fingers delicate and raised like a symphony conductor tracing music in thin air. He's an astronaut in a sad rocket, aiming blindly for the sky. He lurches heavenward. My stomach sinks hollow to the ground, like it does when I reach for a missing wallet or a small hand behind me that isn't there, a paroxysm of fear rising. How his falling is my falling, tethered together like mountain climbers crossing a great crevasse.

I blink, and we are young again, before life required crampons on our boots. Suspended in that sacred place between reality and infinity where things don't fall, where zero gravity holds us together, constant and eternal.

The rocket stops with a jerk, and he's dust again, wandering in the desert land ahead. An unlatched gate between us, swinging open and shut in the wind.

Laundry

Her plastic Kroger bags in the bottom of my cabinet,
smoothed into perfect squares like origami, lost under
a nest of wrinkled ones balled up in my fistful of hurry,
tell me that the art of mothering is knowing how to fold
things right. Basket of neglected garments sits in my
darkest corners, rumpling.

Her fingers like steam rollers finding the right-angle
in any puckered fabric—even pleated skirts, wild
pluming at the hem like undisciplined children
tucked neatly into empty closets.

But, look how the peacock fans her feathers to spread
the air open, how the wind scatters and gathers white
sands into impetuous ripples on the dune. Notice how
receding rivers leave land bars rising like grooved
gullets between channels of water, swallowed.

See the way nature pleats where no fullness is, folding into
an eternal logic of undoing. Mothering, the same infinite
universe oscillating between making and felling, the same

ruinous beauty of it all, unstitching us at the seams—
openings like creased cotton with missing buttons
exposing the tender naked underneath.

Tintern Abbey

> "Metaphysics is a dark ocean without shores
> or lighthouse, strewn with many a
> philosophic
> wreck."
> —Immanuel Kant

cracked paint above a patch of
dried marigolds. the shed roof
stripped of moss, bare as discarded

chicken bones, bleached a pale sand.
a place of shelter blistered naked

clean-carved by sunlit current.
nature folding languid into
heat and hold:

the work of soul is August's
call, it blossoms not but settles
still into routine,

a living prayer—

settled like dust that sinks into
the ruts of shiplap on the old barn.

the old king alone with his
grief, resolve etched into the
furrows of his skin like rippled silt.

tide wrack on the margins of my memory,
clinging like loss in the noontide heat,
emptying me out with the power to
chasten and subdue.

the tepid tide ebbing, pulling me away
from the shore, carrying me like hollow
driftwood across a still and silent sea.

Hosea plays in the rain

Seven days before the first day of summer and it's already 95-degrees.
My yard is teeming with neighborhood girls running with red faces around
an imaginary lagoon of cobalt waters, a mirage as real to you as rain.

You are seven, but you share a birthday with summer and will soon
turn eight. You were born in the desert, which, you say, is why you
love the heat.

But fancy is no match for humidity, and you beg me to douse you with the
garden hose. I think about my budget, not to mention the drought,
before abandoning reason. June is no time for counting.

At first the water hisses and stings your arms with a thousand bug bites.
Then droplets fall like thunder from the nozzle, hitting your head
and the ground with thuds and splats. You squeal as the cold steals your

breath. I imagine steam rising from your hot skin, joy condensing into mist
like a halo of lake fog, illusion becoming solid as droplets of cool water
shimmer in the sunlight before evaporating on the pavement, right before
my eyes.

Extinction

You think you're something else now because,
from the top bunk, your feet almost touch the
ceiling when you stretch your legs above your
head, straight as a compass needle pointing

northward. I think you could dance on top
of the world with those legs, spinning around
your axis across the Ganges while balancing on
toes curled to a pointe like the nose of a river dolphin.

I want to tell you those freshwater dolphins swim
blind and on their side through dim waters,
compelled by distant light and echoes of lost sound,
while the whole world unfurls before you now

like a moonflower. Sometimes I think you radiate
as if lit from within like the Painted Desert when
the light is almost gone and the cliffs turn purple and
glow like the inside of a flame, like a dream.

I remember how, long before we divorced, your dad
and I would drive from Phoenix across the Mogollon
Rim to the Grand Canyon and back in a single day,
and every time I could feel the air getting lighter and

colder the further north we'd go and how I'd press my
nose against the glass of the car window to measure our
progress—just like when I was young, about your same
age now, when your legs are almost long enough to

reach the ceiling. I wonder if you feel like you're
holding up the weight of our world on the bottom
of your feet, the way firstborn daughters do, always
wanting everything right.

That's what I want to say when you summon me a half
hour past bedtime to perform your latest act in the

art of growing up. I want to hold your childhood in my cupped hands and put it in a mason jar with holes in the lid, using its light to find my way.

Instead, I ask how you got so lovely in only eleven years. You smile and pull the moon up to your chin like a blanket, like a dream.

Kayaking

> "I learned not to fear infinity,
> …
> The wheel turning away from itself,
> The sprawl of the wave,
> The on-coming water."
> —Theodore Roethke

Instead of ground
      feel the stirring,
the turning away.

See a fox in the park dart into
a forest of ashes.

These days the things deepest
down are always disappearing
like spindrift—
wilderness,
acts of devotion,

as the angler waits on the shore,
apprentice to the slow dance of
nature
      its long withholding—
      its sudden flourish.

Follow and take the way of the river
through the city,
indeterminate on
tributaries of absence.

Go missing and apostrophize
on ancient waters, cast a line
like a pair of gills, filaments
sifting the current for air.

Watch the kayak upturned,
floating ahead like a promise,

        breath shallow as a
        bluegill out of water

wingbeats quickening in
a flight of tree swallows
approaching a silver sky.

Let it slip away like time
between your fingers,
an epiphany breaking open on
the waves—oars like open doors
reaching out to touch the sea.

Deus Ex Machina

Hot air ripples like water as I bend over
the path, body arcing above the garden,
muscles holding. Summer grows extravagant
as cancer here, pools and quivers on

the brow, wiped away in the still tension
of the work. I tug and pull tufts of grass up
by the roots lodged stubborn in the narrow
cracks where they shouldn't be.

Things always where they shouldn't be
these days like the missing shoe found
submerged under a magnolia tree. Our
good dishes forgotten in the bushes by

the playhouse. Even my anger uprooted
malignant from the deep, fisted wind
howling out of nowhere. Like the day we
hiked to the reservoir, got caught in the

storm and ran faster than thunder.
one one-thousand...
two one-thousand...

I tell the children to count to ten
when anger rises.

But leaves fall like wilted snowflakes
on the lawn and claps of madness bellow
right above our heads. And the grass always
comes back in the cracks of the crooked path,

erasing it. So I keep pulling, trying to outwit
nature, trying to hold us together—my back
the truss of an old bridge, supporting the
weight of the fragile structure. Bent as a

skein of geese searching for good light.
My hands imposing order on the soil,
body arcing like a narrative.

The Milky Way

> "God is a circle whose center is everywhere and circumference nowhere."
> —Empedocles

Not only is marriage about bodies—
sublunary lands mapped
with hands, what lovers
pursue with Euclidean geometry.

More like galaxies,
dust and dark
curved by necessity,
black hole circling
somewhere in the middle
like a heart unbeating.

Yet, from this place just
a swath of stars familiar as
his cotton t-shirt I've washed
a billion times, our mess an
infinity of prime numbers

I fold and unfolded,
fold again like paper
snowflakes.

A dusty mirror,
our ordinary little bedroom,
the road or bridge is

God somehow inside us.
Just as sunlight
is simplified religion.

Marriage, closer to fractals.
Like putting a mountain in
your pocket.

This is partly an erasure poem. Source material: "Mere Christianity," C.S. Lewis. Signature Classics, *The Complete C.S. Lewis*. Pages 128-129.

Clocks

When he comes, he sets my clocks—
the travel alarm I only use if the

power goes out, so old you can
hardly press the buttons down.

The ersatz one in my daughter's
room that resembles an antique

bell-clock. Even the digital numbers
on my coffee pot. I watch him make

his rounds, moving the time with
thumbs certain once as steel.

He'd lift us by those thumbs
when we were small, heaving us

up and down like an oil drill, hands
hanging on for dear life.

What joy we must have felt at the
thought of falling from such heights,

fear of losing time nothing more
than childish folly, as remote to us

as the trembling hands of a longcase
clock in the hallway striking midnight.

Gardensong

> Hosea 2:7
>
> "What does it matter how many
> lovers you have if none of them
> gives you the universe?"
> —Jacque Lacan
>
> ut operaretur eum
> —Voltaire's *Candide*

Desire is taking a picture
of the moon. The trip to faraway
that made you miss your bed,
an apple gone soft.

The way summer fades the
new drapes pooling by the
window-pane. How pain feels
so much like suspense.

And I, thumbing my past
like an old brochure, a native

who knows what the tourist misses:
The country in all seasons. The way
cold light slant on the city bridge

shadows the daily, a garden now
with fields of heather purpling within
its borders. How love is a land in need

of always tilling, promises made of bone,
broken marrow bonds between us. Soil like
hands finally taking what's given—

the rain that will come, a harvest from
sodden ground, backs arched under the
sun, bent over the earth in praise.

The Mistress

I imagine your hair down,
unfastened to let fall like
reaped wheat.

Desert wife, I am to you.
Desirable as a fig tree
out of season, fallow ground.

You are not like us.

Days divided into barley
loaves, we wait like
husbandmen for heavy
loads. Harvest affection,
gather what's given.
Sun-slaked desire,
winnowed.

Need articulates our
nights, restless children
climbing into our marital
beds, parting them like the Red Sea.

Your heart an abandoned well,
a window left open to the dark.

What I hide in the day like
a nursing baby, you bare open
in the shadow; while I hope,

you slip past the threshing
floor unnoticed, trace dirt paths
down further.

Your body an aquifer
instead. My lover with
hands to your earth

divining water, your edges
smoothed by the
taking, the running over.

Same as the way I sweep
dirt into the corners of
my kitchen. Dig moats
in all the sand. How I

search for rivers in my own body,
striking stone like arid bone,
looking for a current to carry me.

Sinuous rills taking me away
to the sea, as if they could
save me.

Against Love Poetry

after Eavan Boland

Hosea 3:1

Instead, say to your sons and daughters, *I will love your mother*. Sleep, still, on your side of the bed. Leave her coffee in the morning. Take back the times she wasn't enough, reverse and eat all the suppers she didn't prepare. Call her by your name, your father's same, this bride-ghost of your youth. Return to the thicket and cut back the forest, refusing the welter of its jungle. Find strength in the work. Dig and place anemone on the banks of some trackless field, covering like a shroud over your past. Plant autumn crocus, some flowering hyssop. Make room for new growth. Go to her again and confess your indifference, beat your wild heart like a tabor until a new song is heard.

Love anyway the one who loves you less. Bury your body like a root and wait for it to grow into an oak. Find shade from the branches and carve hope into its trunk like permanent initials. When she leaves, wait for the rain, and say to the children, *I will love your mother.*

The Good Snake

It resembled a strip of tar paper, basking on the patio in the white light of my fear. No coincidence it came on the longest day of the year. I know all about them, heard the cornpone advice, how they take the bad things in the garden so best to compromise. Bargain with danger, a kind of kickback from nature. But there in all the wildness deep down it makes me shudder, this hitchhiker on my daily commute, this skinny-dipper streaking bareback across my morning.

I've contended with wilderness before on this patch of city ground at the bottom of a hill: English ivy wrapping its fingers in a chokehold around the Rose of Sharon, the privet's cancerous reign. Gullies running serpentine beneath the foundation. Or the time a baby snake, circling like a drain, settled in my boot's dank basement, an electric sock balled up in the toe.

I've read they swallow prey whole: victims like hikers betrayed by a narrow mountain crevasse, hearts shifting to make room for the kill, conformed to a bottleneck of abyss.

And yet, my heart. This too an omen, its own dark forest coiled to strike.
How the force that tethers us, keeps us from spinning, sends also the floodwaters. This treaty with gravity, the weight of it holding, a wedding vow for better or worse.

Theodicy

The katydid startled me as I opened the door,
his leaf-like lamina wings attached to a spine of stem.

He had already wandered into the poison,
my defense against the darkness,
so I buried him under a roof of pine straw.

Sometimes the wrong thing gets broken,
like the eighty-year-old pane of glass I
cracked with the neck of a broom handle,
swatting an errant wasp.

My dad would have grabbed it with a paper towel,
breaking it between his fingers. But I think too much
about Murphy's Law.

I think about it all: frames with missing windows,
bugs interred in dust balls in the corner,
the thin separation between us and nature.

I have a recurring dream where I can't find my room,
lost in a blank maze of hotel corridors. It's how I imagine myself
growing old, fumbling around in the dark for doors that no longer

open, memories like maple roots letting go of the earth and
rising blindly towards the pale light, unanchored.

The dream began after my husband
lost his mind (it seemed) and left.

Anything that can happen will.

Maybe it was gravity, not villainy, that made him go;
maybe I wandered into the poison he put out in fear,
armor in that terrible war with himself.

Maybe it was just my turn to be on the wrong side of
the glass. My time to feel the weight of being broken,
like the hull of a fallen limb, torn from our giant red oak
by the wind, that I'll use as kindling when the cold comes back.

Fixer-Upper

"Why do the wrong things grow here," I spit, prying weeds elbow-high from the flower bed out front, the one next to the bald spots in the grass, thanks to last year's drought. I'm a Pharisee imposing order, tucking, smoothing the corners. But it looks more like a brothel at my feet.

Was it Blake who said the road of excess leads to the palace of wisdom? Maybe I'll let those tufts of chickweed alone, wild toupees littering my lawn. Pluck the morning from its crabapple stem instead, pillage a quorum of native daisies. Buttercup blossoms will be my yellow road, my primrose path of indiscretion. I'll boil bitterroot like a prophet, leave the day unmade as tousled covers. Blow dandelion seeds to tell time.

I'll watch my work rise like hot air rendering thunder, ditches turning into rivers, rivers becoming law. *See how it all goes to hell anyway?* Even the riverbank's high ground, breaking way. Nothing's sacred. Not our bodies, just annuals, just tempests for a time.

That jungle is the only thing here that will last. See it prune me back to wonder? Just now the pale madwort greens the rock and crevice, saplings sprout like circus wishes in impossible places while ivy juts its tendrils through my window frame. It's futile to match their wits.

I'll sit here under its bramble, a roof blooming of blackberry. Braid white clover into crowns. See the neighbors stare, pointing like green thumbs from atop their emerald lawns? They are wrecked by beauty.

God Speaks

for the single mothers

"So I took them out of the land of Egypt
and brought them into the wilderness."
—Ezekiel 20:10

Not the burning bush but the sprig of crabgrass in the asphalt. When epiphany is an eclipse of light around my doorjamb. The string of spider web that levitates like an empty clothesline ghosting my garden. The day I found the pressed penny buried like a fossil in carpet lint, the one from the dinosaur museum a decade ago, when pockets were portals. Her baby tooth I keep like a wish tucked inside the seashell stranded on the kitchen windowsill. God spoke the summer the children saved a baby turtle in our yard. He spoke when we sent it back into the wild.

The Prophet

I'm rinsing dirty cups when I glance outside the
kitchen window—the one facing the patio
flanked by vines with wild tendrils, a copse of

native azaleas, ivy swallowing a shipwrecked
birdbath in the corner—the patio with a crack
running reptile across the cement where the earth

below it sank. This old house. Too many hollow
places, like the gulley beneath the root cellar that
swells with spring groundwater. Or the inside

of the tire swing that fills with rain and turns to rust.
I fear hidden spaces like I do old oaks with heavy
limbs, empty with decay. I wonder what might

happen on our worst day. Then it catches my eye,
a linear flash of light midair, a beam of reflection
floating. I stop and study the air. A breeze lifts a

diaphanous string of silk suspended like a tightrope
across my patio floor with no beginning or end,
just a middle. The light skips across it, center balancing

before shifting into transparency again, an apparition.
I recall the times I've walked into a spider web,
the thing I couldn't see, frantic to escape the

feeling of wool on virgin skin. But for today I am a prophet.
I only see light dancing on silence, the beauty of the peril.

Eight

Always the downy cloud, crayon-sky vision of lateral precision, mistaking fancy for nature. Never blank space or stones protruding from the grass like icebergs.

Always the beginning and never the three-dimensional middle, dark as an urban river or the thick smoke that trails the big rig on its way to the paper mill on Wednesday—eclipse of smog circling a cloudy eye like perspective.

Never the blind curve but the desert road rippling towards the destination like a ribbon, the ribbon without the knot in the center pried loose with serrated scissors, sharp as a tongue.

Never indifference but the penetrating gaze still fascinated. Always moving water and never detritus, the damnation of things left behind.

Always the blessing and never the prayer, its delicate husk discarded.

Always the single flower with a spherical center, violet world contained with boat-like petals. While a pair of wings fly under a crescent sun in the corner—eternal yellow, always summer.

The Anniversary

Remember how we used to love?

The way our hearts were rough-hewn
and rabbeted together like the shiplap
on the barn out back, the one you
built by hand?

How we filled it long ago not with
living things, but all the stuff we
couldn't hold—your grandmother's
sideboard, boxes of china overflowing,
all kindling now in a vacant forest.

The yoke was never light,
but we plowed good ground,
cultivated a modest garden.

We live on idle acres now,
hearts prone to wander vine to vine
in an incomprehensible jungle.

Who can tell where the wilderness
begins or end these days? Declension
is our portion, atonement for our sins,
a kind of cosmic logic.

And what do they say about
how we unloved? How it fell apart
like loose boards until all became
unfettered beats into the wind,
almost like wings?

How the roof was first to go, and when
it went, how big was the sky,
home eclipsed by branches wild, so full
we no longer needed rooms to grow?

On Learning Einstein Was Divorced on Valentine's Day

February 14, 2016

In this age of down-pulling and disbelief, as Carlyle once said,
let me wax poetic about the universe, offer some profundity
about love's power, like the story of the couple on my local news.
Widowed and wizened, set up on a blind date and eventually married,
despite all logic and reason.

Let me try to capture the miracle of being found and chosen,
a universe of epic intention. To offer, like Blake, some vision
that life is not a mill with complicated wheels, Newtonian gears
of clockwork steel governed by law and probability.

Today, of all days, let me believe in the music of gravitational
waves, time folded within the romance of black holes circling—
the improbability of sound rippling from darkness into primeval
whispers, saying to us now, *this is the beginning.* Like a box of
letters discovered in the stardust of attics.

Let me find in the mapping of the universe the cartography of
my own wild heart, refusing to believe in nothing. Bent but not broken,
a relic held in chambers deep as sea caves wreathed in light, an apostle
beating its wings against the night.

Gomer Goes Home

I try to pray when northern winds persist,
refuse the cries mewling on marshlands
frosted thick.

Silence falling on deaf ears
asleep on stone pillows.

The nadir of a setting sun sole unit of measurement
in this country,

monarchies of ice.

"I will bring you back to this land."

Apostasy like walking in water fully clothed,
           unnatural as childbirth,
           remote as a Lapland fell.

I hear the children on the path flanked
                         by
                             cloudberries,
                    amber pale as the
                    hull of an ark.

Here, where soon the sun-torched rim of day
will set open into night, this edge of earth
pulsing electric with light—

kingdoms boundless as the breezes blown
through mountain ash, heather purpling in
brooms that sweep the moorlands wild

with harebells; even the melancholy thistle
on roadside verges will come

after this mile of winter before dawn.

Entropy

*At what point could you be any less true
and still be you?*

In September she wakes to an early
chill, pulls time up from the
bottom of the bed warm as a quilt.

Leaves rustle like crisp, starched skirts,
worn threads unravelling their green.

And she dreams of letting her hair go
gray while an old oak scatters seeds,
giving away a measure of her load;
acorns falling like discarded corsets.

She holds onto the weight of it—
visits arid peaks, builds cairns
of upland rock bare as bone
but sleeps in valleys where rivers

rush deep towards some incomprehensible
loss; children draped on memory like
mist, gossamer covering what prospers
with a veil of antique lace.

But how easily the mayfly sheds
desire in a halo of lake fog like
vestigial wings; whirlybirds falling
naked in the stream while a harvest

moon unbuttons on the dark. And
see how time slips down to the foot
of her bed with wrinkled sheets, while
she dreams of dropping leaves wearing
nothing but pale skin.

I Write

Sometimes, just because it's Wednesday.
This time of year, since trees are empty coat
racks and the lines deepening between my eyebrows
resemble bird tracks in the snow.

I write even though I paint a hoary sky with tinted water,
boil chicken bones for supper. Walk the dogs counterclockwise.
Pry my daughter's miniature teacups from the sink disposal.

Because the boy has never stayed.

(unlike the scene in *Love Actually* where
Colin Firth lets his words float away in lake water,
choosing the Portuguese lover instead).

I write while the children bicker over cardboard boxes
and I hear news of the royal engagement.
Young Windsors having brunch with
the Queen.

Because my age feels suddenly like misfortune.
The day after Christmas. Scraping dishes from a
holiday meal. Desire sealed up in Tupperware containers
inside the deep freezer.

Since life in sum total is more *Othello* than *Twelfth Night*.

I write to have a good name, eternal as those Riace bronzes,
Greek warriors raised from a grave of dirty
dishwater, greater part earthly or divine?

Perhaps to crumple my youth like a first draft and hurl
it at the bloody universe. Toss the scraps ahead
like crumbs. Keep writing my way back whole.

All the Light

Look. All the light there is to see
is here sometimes, it seems.
Even on an every-other Friday
when we exchange the girls near
the airport in the rain and the sky
is flat as a cotton sheet. I watch
planes disappear into the clouds as if
taken by covers. As if God opened his
mouth and swallowed.

I've watched planes land not
far from here with my father,
sitting on the hood of his car
outside the runway like rednecks
at the theater. Even now that noise
I hear, seconds when so much
sound became silence. He worked
around jets for 40 years, which
is why, he says, he now can't hear
a damn thing.

But Beethoven wrote his masterpiece
while nearly deaf. Never married,
he lost his hearing by 46. I'm 46, and
sometimes my body feels unnecessary
when I'm lost in a poem or song,
myth and marvel eclipsing sense.
Simple objects rendered unordinary:
a chain-link fence, a car door closing.
Home a *turbulent democracy*
of little hills, C.S. Lewis once said.

Look here, I want to say, and
imagine all the mountains you hoped
to see close as acre and plow on the
patio outside our kitchen window.
Travel the world like a mote of dust

floating in the sunlight.
Dip your hands like oars into
the dirty dishes, let the gravy
boat sink to the bottom, its china
hull filling with water before
draining, a ship resurrected with
no treasure.

All the light there is to see is here
sometimes, inside raindrops
beading my string of patio lights.
Even the LED tealight, glowing like
foxfire, burning flameless as first love
in this land of always longing.

Beethoven was inspired by Friedrich
Schiller's poem "Ode to Joy":
May he who has had the fortune to gain
a true friend/And he who has won a
noble wife/Join in our jubilation!

Jubilation must be what the great
composer felt the night he conducted
his ninth symphony for the first time.
So hard of hearing, the story goes,
and so transported, he got a few
measures behind and didn't realize
the moment was over.

Just imagine. Did you know this
would have been (coincidentally)
our jubilee year?

These things I ponder after
the latest kid exchange in the
rain, as you whiz past in the
left lane. Your Ford F-150,
Georgia-bulldog red, taking
you to God knows where.

The spray from your tires,
contrails streaming from behind,
makes it hard for me to see. Until the
windshield wipers spring like
giant hands searching for the
right key. A song traced in thin air.

Kingdom Come

Job 38:31

Fall is late this year, so much
warmer than most we can recall,
and a record drought. We wring
our hands and doubt.

Dust covers dry creek beds
while wildfires simmer beyond
the ridge, glowing like the open
burner on an electric stove, radiant
light against a blacktop sky.

We see the horizon burning as we top
the highway hill, mistaking it for a
lingering sunset; so pretty, my daughters
say. Homes gone up in flames, I fear.

I think about a pretty poem I just read,
the poet capturing all I wanted to say
about how much of life is grace,
while hillside in the dust I labor on.

How easy is this regret, to see my
losses like wrong words erased
on the page, contentment's
scattered ashes circling in the wind.

How hard is praise when time
resists my will, when the castles I
build smolder on the ridge.

Not long now before first frost
will cover all these faults, the
bands of Orion cinching the sky
as if to testify,

thy will be done.

While hillside in the dust huntsmen
pursue their burning hearts, carry the
burden of their days and say,
once, I was here.

Atlantis

"Because, what if they don't turn out okay?" The question, posed by my 14-year old daughter, hung in the air as we drove past the park after school late one afternoon. I was talking about motherhood, and she matter-of-factly justified her plan to forgo having children. Too much risk, she implied. Somewhere around middle school, my fiery and impetuous toddler became a politic young woman, cautious and so careful. My eyes scanned the park to our west that only days before was submerged under flood waters from the nearby river, its banks swollen bellies giving way under the pressure of record rains, turning the adjacent landscape into an ancient swamp navigable only by kayaks or canoes—to me, enchanted as the lost city of Atlantis. Now, the waters were receding, and we glanced in unison to see the place resuming its ordinary shape and symmetry, paths and benches reemerging, fields again visible but dotted with impromptu islands.

Her question lingered unanswerable, replaced by more linear subjects: what to do for dinner, her geometry test the next day. My mind wandered to Plato as we pulled into the Chick-fil-a drive-thru, how he believed math could solve the secrets of the universe. I tossed the loose change into the cupholder with old receipts as we headed toward home, and we wondered when it would rain again. Our future unpredictable as a body of water, incalculable as the hope of mythic lands.

Empty Nesting

This copper fungus
whorling the wood in the
garden like a newborn's grip

wasn't there last week,
and the gardenia blooms that
have sprung out of everywhere
make me wonder: if I looked
close enough, could I watch them
spread open?

Already the children sleep late on
Christmas morning. Already the new
fiddleleaf fig has outgrown its pot
while greenbrier vines twine the
shrubbery like an invasion of the
body snatchers.

Even now the patch of fallow
ground I cleared out by the
cottonwoods has a canopy
fit for a hobbit and the hydrangeas

we just planted last fall have
already unfurled their glory, blue
umbrellas raised like objections in

the rain. I dream a herd of mule deer
prunes back the years along with
the milkweed, unbeads the barberry
brambles like our days. I dream

I chase fireflies into a night dark
as a mouth, look for seeds of
saplings between its teeth, reach for
things I can still hold in my hands.

The Law of Falling Bodies

James Robert Nicholson Crea
1934-2021

James Edward Crea
1856-1937

Galileo said we can know the time it will take an object to
fall from any height. His elegant formula
a way to cope with a world that breaks our hearts,

some measure of control over the chaos, an equation
of our losses. When my father falls again,
I do the math, count the distance between my birth and his.

Those 37 the same number of years between her and me,
my youngest teenage Einstein who thinks
we're light years apart and falling at relative speeds. To her, what she is

must have nothing to do with me, as if she's infinity.
But I can see, like those number-pattern problems
on the SAT, how it will go. How my father's namesake, great uncle Jim,

died in 1937 at the same hospital of the same thing as him.
How in 37 years more I'll be the same age
as my father and she the same as I when he died.

No black holes between us like galaxies. Generations close
as linens on a line, years constant as a sequence
of prime numbers connected at the corners with only a clothespin.

Lives caught in a sudden upturn of wind like blankets
falling, billowing towards an end folded over end folded over end.

This Persistent Gravity

for M&M

If the tailorbird can sew leaves together
with spider web silk and its beak,
we can learn to fix the toilet that whistles.

And if the darkling beetle can live in the desert
by harvesting fog with its hydrophilic wings,
there's beauty in what you've been given:

a single mother.
A world that sinks and sags like my shoulders.

Yes, some days the gleaming sea.
But mostly we're fishing boats climbing waves,
wing flutter against a wake.

Certain lessons will be easy, you see,
like knowing Jeff Buckley's version of
"Hallelujah" is the best, but other things
will always confound us:

physics,
boys. Why boys become
men that rivers take for no reason.

How rivers were
once just melting snow.

Did I ever tell you my first boyfriend,
Mike, died in his sleep when he was 36?
His own lungs a deep river.

He gave me my first kiss when I was
only 14, sitting on the side of his bed
under a strobe light he kept in his room
(God knows why), and every time we
kissed, the room was lit a different color.

I'm sorry, but you will likely inherit
the blue spider veins that circumnavigate
my legs like rivers.

And if you were going to get my
bird-egg blue eyes,
you would've by now

not that they would be enough anyway
to make this darkling world of rivers and
spider veins and ex-boyfriends okay.

Listen. Goodness is a recessive trait.
You'll only have the umbrella when
you don't need it.

We never get to where we think we need to go.

No inner circle or distant planet here,
just circles in circles inside of circles
that pulse and spin like disco lights
(maybe a black hole)
tornadoes for sure

toilets that whistle.

You'll get all kinds of advice,
like measure success by its circumference,
take what makes you feel better.

But nothing will stop the hard days
gathering ahead like a congregation
of barn swallows.

Even now, my blue eyes are
my only things I can't find fault with,
and I did not give those to you

just the spider veins.

You'll think that all sundry of things
might fix it, the ache reminding you
what you're not, what you need to do to matter.

One day it will even wake you in the night,
your heart shaking like wings in a tree. Every boy
you'll ever want partly some attempt to make everything
okay.

Look. Once upon a time, the universe was empty,
dust and dark spinning, like those roundabouts
at the park, pushing everything from the center, pushing
everything off.

We're all dust sewn together by a single thread of light,
life still all that dust falling away from a center,
our faces pockmarked by stars.

Love is the leaning in, this persistent gravity.
It's the centripetal force, like a mother's hand
somehow always on our back, steadying,
holding us on.

Hosea, Single

In January your keys keep the time,
plink like antlers discarded in the foyer.

House sealed tight as a covenant. I hold
our truth with baby-fisted certainty, days

stacked neatly as closed books on a calendar.
Hours like the travel of the front porch rocker.

In March, the month for war, you leave me.
Reverse-alchemy. Gold, like youth, returned to dross.

I start to date, trace the river after a hard rain,
mud-soak wash churning towards some lighted place.

Winter drags its elegy across an orchid sky,
spring's slow reckoning. Peace like sleep;

nothing for fitful years then at once pulled under
in the mock-drop of dream, arms and legs detached

from my body. Mornings I am a crescent moon
curled around the horizon of a vacant bed, a

bookend alone in a storefront window. Single as
a prophet sent to strange lands, chosen for signs

and wonders. Revelation comes quiet as the stray
cat on my porch, arched back rubbing sleep from

the corners of my mind. I turn April's white-blank
page—from aperire, meaning, *to open.*

Angie Crea O'Neal's work has appeared in *Sycamore Review, The Christian Century, The Windhover, Cumberland River Review*, and elsewhere. She teaches English at Shorter University in Rome, Georgia, where she lives with her daughters.

www.ingramcontent.com/pod-product-compliance
Lightning Source LLC
Chambersburg PA
CBHW030225170426
43194CB00007BA/860